HHB

Turtle Island
Tree
Psalms

Poems by
Hugh Ogden

HHB

Higganum Hill Books : Higganum, Connecticut

First Edition
First Printing September 1, 2006

Higganum Hill Books
P.O. Box 666, Higganum, CT 06441
Phone (860) 345-4103
Email: rcdebold@mindspring.com

Library of Congress Control Number: 2006010930
ISBN10: 0-9776556-2-8
ISBN13: 978-0-9776556-2-5

Frontispiece: <u>Mondrian, Piet</u> *Gray Tree* , 1911 Oil on canvas

Library of Congress Cataloging-in-Publication Data

Ogden, Hugh, 1937-
  Turtle Island tree psalms : poems / by Hugh Ogden. -- 1st ed.
    p. cm.
  ISBN 0-9776556-2-8 (alk. paper)
  1. Nature--Poetry. 2. Trees--Poetry. I. Title.
  PS3565.G383T87 2006
  811'.54--dc22

                                                    2006010930

Independent Publishers Group distributes Higganum Hill Books.
Phone: (800) 888-4741   www.ipgbook.com
Printed in the United States of America.

ACKNOWLEDGEMENTS:

Early versions of these poems appeared in the following periodicals:

CONNECTICUT REVIEW:
"How The White Pine Grieves"
"Yellow Birch, The Driveway Up From The Landing"
"White Cedar, A Medicine Chest Beside Oquossoc Waters"

ART FROM CONNECTICUT FORESTS
(CT Dept. Environmental Protection Brochure
Celebrating 100th Anniversary Purchase of
Meshomasic State Forest):
"White Oak, Meshomasic State Forest"

MIPO (www.mipo@hotmail.com):
"Cottonwood, Piney Creek Before It Enters The Powder"

ODISSEA (trans.into Italian, Donatella Bisutti):
"Sugar Maple, The Cemetary Outside Of Oquossoc"
"Beech, Red Hill, My Roots"
"White Cedar Looking West Towards Mooselook: Its Witness"

TESTIMONIAL VOLUME NEW ORLEANS HURRICANE:
"The Oldest Willow In The Willow Draw Near The Tongue"

Virginia Dehn's painting, "Spirit," appears on the cover of *TURTLE ISLAND TREE PSALMS*. Losing her eyesight and fearful of not being able to work at her easel, Virginia killed herself on July 26, 2005. I'm thankful that her executor, Ginny Connors, granted permission to use "Spirit" as the cover for this book. Every tree in *TURTLE ISLAND TREE PSALMS* speaks the words of my heart: thank you, Virginia, for your paintings, friendship inspiration, and love.

I'm grateful to the MacDowell Colony, the Island Institute in Sitka, Alaska, the Fondation Ledig-Rowohlt (Le Château de Lavigny in Switzerland), and the Ucross Foundation for artist residencies. My heartfelt thanks to Ralph H. Emerson for his knowledge about linguistics and place-names, and to Herman Asarnow, Russ Brooks, Arthur Feinsod, Steve Foley, Susan Kinsolving, Bob Frazer, Joan Malerba-Foran, Kathryn Shaw, and Ruth Woodcock who helped me with these poems or were my inspiration, and to Benjamin, Katya, Amelia, Theo, Aaron, Josh and Scott.

To all my spirit guides, especially Soge, Dutch, Skip, and the Friends of Hartford Monthly Meeting: I'm still listening.

CONTENTS

PRELUDE

The Voice Of Earth   3

PSALMS

Lodgepole By The Medicine Wheel   6
White Cedar, A Medicine Chest Beside Oquossoc Waters   8
Box Elder By Clear Creek   10
Cottonwood, Piney Creek Before It Enters The Powder   12
Sumac, The Floodplain, Nayaug   14
White Birch Sapling In Peat Beside Gray Water, Oquossoc 15
Silver Maple Rooted Through A Granite Crevice Cupsuptic 16
Plum, The Orchard In The Wassuc Hills   17
Shagbark Above An Oxbow In The Connecticut   18
Apple In The Orchard Off The Turnpike, Naubuc   20
Red Pine, A Cathedral Pine Near Eustis   22
Hemlock By A Writer's Studio Above
     The Connecticut   23
Locust, The Rock Garden, Chestnut Hill Road   25
Douglas Fir, The Inland Passage, Kilkatla   26
Walnut To Whitman In Camden Cemetery, A Leaf Of
     Regret?   28
Turtle Island Chestnut Near Dock Ruins, Nayaug   29
Mountain Laurel, Little Moose Mountain,
     The Adirondacks   30
Elm: What It Should Have Meant To Be An American
     in 2003   31
Black Spruce Bucked And Piled Outside The Kitchen
     Window, Oquossoc   32
Ash, Wassuc   35
Tamarack, Oquossoc   36
Alder, Stabilizing Soil, Narramantic Island   37
White Birch Leaning Over The Outhouse, Oquossoc   38
White Oak, Meshomasic State Forest   39

Poplar, South Bog, Oquossoc   40
Fir Brushing The Screen Of The Living Room Window,
    Naubuc   41
Aspen Below Kachina Peak   42

INTERLUDE: A RESPONSORY

A Two-legged Falls For Trees   44
How The White Pine Grieves   45
When Trees Stop Talking   46
High Plains Dialogue   48

PSALMS

Weeping Birch, The Lodge Below The Big Horns   50
Box Elder By Piney Creek   51
Cottonwood, Where Clear Creek Joins Piney   52
The Oldest Willow In The Willow Draw
    Near The Tongue   53
White Pine, The Guardian, Route 17   55
Fir On The Oquossoc Shore, Singing   56
Beech, The Red Hill Bluff Above The Connecticut,
    How I Sustain You   57
Yew In The Cemetery, Naubuc   58
Hornbeam, The West Shore Of The Island,
    January, 2004   59
White Oak, Red Hill Overlooking Nayaug   60
Fir by The Porch, Listening   61
Mountain Ash, Growing By The Fallen Down Shed   62
Beech in A Grove, Red Hill, My Roots   63
Black Oak Beside A Midden Mound, Red Hill   64
Peach, The Orchard Behind The Cider Mill   65
Sugar Maple, The Cemetery Outside of Oquossoc   66
Yellow Birch, The Driveway Up From The Landing   67
Bing Cherry, The Orchard By Lake Erie   68
White Cedar Looking West Towards Mooselook:
    Its Witness   69

Pin Cherry Under Fir And Spruce, Oquossoc   70
Fir Sapling, Aziscohos After Clear Cutting   71
Pear Looking East Above The Connecticut   72
Rhododendron, Oquossoc, By The Cabin   74
Red Oak Rooted On Red Hill Above The Floodplain   76
White Pine, After Living A Hundred Years Looking
          West Across The Lake   77

CODA

Earth Voice   79

Trees are our relatives – we call them 'tall standing brothers.'
    –Bear Heart–

There is no death in mortal things, and no end in ruinous
death. There is only mingling and interchange of parts, and it
is this that we call 'nature.'
    –Empedocles–

Go to the pine if you want to learn about the pine. ...You
must leave your subjective preoccupation with yourself.
Otherwise you impose yourself on the object and do not
learn.
    –Basho–

A fool sees not the same tree that a wise man sees.
    –Blake–

for Elizabeth Tiedens

and to the memory of
Virginia Dehn

Prelude

The Voice Of Earth
(think, thank: IE tong)

I think in veins deep down,
in standing stones, mountains

and plains, spin the web of
sea and land that is the globe,

the generation and ground of
being. All roots feed from me

and go back to food. Air my
protection. Rivers, oceans,

and rain my blood, my nerves
all creatures. All things

that move, even continents,
vibrate with my thinking,

giving back what was given,
rising from what has returned,

the gratitude of thought.
Most who live on me know this:

spruce, ponderosa, birch
and others who speak these

psalms, four-leggeds, many-
leggeds, winged feather-

creatures soaring above,
even some two-leggeds who

respect the ground they walk
on: they also have a mind.

Psalms

Lodgepole By The Medicine Wheel

When you're stricken because your
beloved has died, find a foot trail

to the Big Horns. Follow the path
up the north spur to where I've been

growing so many years, to stones
that make spokes, hub, a wheel.

Stand beside me, don't try to speak.
Let your body cast a shadow as mine

does, be another gnomon on the dial
that clocks seasons, exits, earth–

sounds growing new skin. Your shadow
will remember declensions of love,

feel deepening declinations of land,
tell the angle and circumference of

your care, every minute of attention,
each blessed second of sun and shadow

you had together, irreplaceable
hours of embodied joy, and point

to how you can know what is really
here: in cold space sage-sticks

twined on a juniper, six prayer
ribbons woven with names of spirit-

guides hanging in my needles, your
beloved infolded deep below axle

and rim into what was here before
the universe began, our shadows

pointing behind us, before, beyond.

White Cedar, A Medicine Chest Beside Oquossoc Waters

If you don't know
how to heal, walk
to the lake edge

where I'm growing.
Kneel in the snow
and look for shreddy

bark by my trunk.
If you don't find
any, dig a little

and believe. Trust
what your fingers
touch. Dig deeper.

When the next-door
widow limps over
to ask what you're

doing tell her
the truth: you don't
know but maybe spirits

will soothe the knee
she hurt coming
down an ice-slick

driveway yesterday.
Invite her indoors
to taste the cup

of tea I told you
how to prepare
from bark-shreds

because it heals
broken dreams, your
doubt, and her bones.

Box Elder By Clear Creek

The wind having dried up old snow
at my feet, the turkey people meet

in council: a child is laid out under
a cottonwood, her fluff-wing broken.

The medicine turkey rubs her wing
with sage, walks away, and lays

a feather on the stone of the ages.
She limps to join him. Now the stone

has a halo and speaks as only a stone
can, long vowels of muffled basalt:

'You have given me of yours and this
feather will massage my wounds even

as you massaged a wing.' The other
turkey people look with gratitude

to the sky and go back to picking
up grain while the medicine turkey

leaves a clump of hay beside what
has suffered, offers a prayer and

the little turkey turns into one
of my children, a box elder leaning

across bottom land blown free of
snow and fertile with wet earth.

Cottonwood, Piney Creek Before It Enters The Powder

I'm at home in wet bottom
lands where so many have
settled, four-leggeds, two-

leggeds, drifting cotton-
fluff aflurry in spring,
where teeth have crunched

grass and defeat has re-
surrected spirits. You can
understand what we say

by putting your ear to
the ground even when autumn
has accepted snow-cover,

the almost beat of flake
after flake, and later when
snow runs liquid as brook

and creek-notes flush their
song. Here in Wyoming and
everywhere words are sown

in an earth containing
all utterance: forgotten
names, lost languages,

sentences spoken from
the heart or carelessly,
even cries of pain because

these alluvial soils of
the Piney archive the ancient
and about to be, provide

a bed which germinates all
language-seeds, everything
you hear when you kneel.

Sumac, The Floodplain, Nayaug

In spring a cluster of stems
and green beginnings, awakenings

out of a peat-bed by the river,
in autumn a candelabra of dun-

scarlet risen from my mother
root, red-umber candle-stalks

that are cut, trimmed, and used
as walking sticks by the elderly

who live on higher ground: I give
them a third leg and faith in

the autumnal radiance earth holds.

White Birch Sapling In Peat Beside Gray Water, Oquossoc

(tree, true: IE deru)

My elders taught me that
to be true to who I am

I had to become a birch.
They said in the long

ago the word 'true' was
the word for tree, so to

be true I had to become
what I am and root beside

your house, just as you
to be human must be who

you are by honoring and
rooting in the humus from

which you came, humility
that true-fertile soil.

Silver Maple Rooted Through A Granite Crevice, Cupsuptic

When you measure me
measure gentleness
if you can, the frail
timbre of leaf sound
in late autumn when,
after wind dies, my
green turns silver-
yellow and brown before
falling, measure stem-
cling and leaf-touch
because even my rough
bark holds by a whisper
and treats the air
as it would a sister.
You might understand
more of who you are
if you understand me,
know more about links
and passages, you in
this quick world just
once, though possibly
again, and knowing that,
more gentle and rooted.

Plum, The Orchard In The Wassuc Hills

If you forget don't worry,
I'm growing near. Even in
winter my limbs, twigs,
and roots prepare flowers

which purple into ovals
absorbing all you think
about or want to do, every-
thing that runs from your

mind: lost objects, ideas,
even generations before
you walked on earth, plumb
flesh under green hung

from hardwood and leaves.
Everything you forget I
store in my pit until it
grows liquid-yellow under

blue, the unconscious, for-
gotten, because we are family
and glow sweet-violet in
the sisterhood of light.

17

Shagbark Above An Oxbow In The Connecticut

I feel for fissures in this
granite outcrop, root through

strands of loam in fractured
rock, spread tuber-hair through

soil-dark decay, the way your
mind, after being locked in

fashion and habit, heals it-
self by finding cracks in

civilization, after thinking
abstractly under clocked

agendas returns to what it
has always been, an inter-

change of water, darkness,
and sun, a simple awareness.

Just like me when I spread
rhizomes around soil particles,

your mind becomes whole when
it roots in the underworld,

reclaims its birthright by
reaching into dark for water

and mineral, into sky for
air and light, repairs broken

connections by growing under
the rainbow of four directions

and living through time's
circle, its health restored

by what is above and below
the oxbow-flood at my feet.

Apple In The Orchard Off The Turnpike, Naubuc
(You shall not eat of the fruit of the tree
which is in the midst of the garden –
Genesis, III, 3, RSV)

Because I was sacred to the Celts,
Christians called me the tree

of knowledge. They were terrified
of people who didn't believe

what they believed so they made
the taste of vitamin-tang and

mineral the act of disobedience,
criminalized what is rounded

by skin and season. You have to
go beyond tradition to enjoy

plump flesh, ignore the sinful
and illicit to be nourished by

mcoun, winesap, and macintosh,
cinnamon-sweet fruit ripened in

temperate zones everywhere on
earth and here on this Connecticut

hill overlooking a deep river
valley that runs down worn

centuries of granite bringing
apple knowledge to a garden.

Red Pine, A Cathedral Pine Near Eustis

If you have to find God
in the sky let her be
a raindrop, a flood of
mist, a snow flake or
the wind. If you don't

find her and still believe
she's somewhere check
the land and oceans. She
can be, if you wish, one
of the Blue Mountains,

the Penobscot or any other
brown river, an ash leaf,
a blade of grass, or
the path worn by your
ancestors into mulched

foot signs, the red fox
slipping from the garden
with a vole. If you have
to find God somewhere let
her be a thing 'thinging'

this world, not your psyche
projected on the sky.
Let her accompany you
gravely, offer the power
and glory of what is.

Hemlock By A Writers' Studio Above The Connecticut

I'm a life-giving shade
beyond your windowpane
who never stops murmuring,

even during winter. My
boughs come from the deep
and my leaves cling flat

to their twigs in a splay
of many hands with life-
lines in each palm, like

the hand Keats offers any-
one who reads or listens,
his "living hand, now warm

and capable" with the same
number of small bones in
it as in any. See, after

a storm as snow slides
off and my branches rise,
I hold a bough toward

you above your window-
sill, needle-veins a-
quiver in the tiny wind,

the green healing shade
of my soul that helps you
read the world's hornbook.

Locust, The Rock Garden, Chestnut Hill Road

I'm a glutton for bark, for a lumped,
leathery cloak which provides hope

for all who come by for tulips, mums,
and iris, even the despair people who

hang their heads and don't look up.
I bump them under ground and come

up through their soles to give them
protection, grow rind to show everyone

how a new coat and skin offer a chance
for the tomorrow that completes a circle.

Douglas Fir, The Inland Passage, Kilkatla

I have little to help you
through the terror and

despair of history, no balm,
can't help the pain of

knowing what has happened
or of being broken, though

the rain and mist have
helped me to live when I

hear cargo-passings over
water, barges of old-growth

cedar and spruce diesel-
rumbling on the way to mills,

when I feel the tight bite
of teeth in friends who

have grown beside me for
centuries, feel the plumb

crash of brothers and sisters.
Come to me even so and share

my strength so you'll know
what it means to survive

generations of your kind,
the solitude of night giving

somber dark to my green
boughs against the fog-misty

background of those no
longer here, my children,

parents, siblings, who have
been felled and slashed.

Walnut To Whitman In Camden Cemetery, A Leaf Of Regret?

When you sang the broadax you knew
that sassafras, hickory, and I
had spirits but sang anyway, sang

the steel-honed edge that slashes
what it wants. You praised muscles
that try to measure all things,

the ax that felled the ancient
and mature, even saplings of Ohio,
Michigan, Indiana, the blind swing

of faith in two-leggeds who cleared
everything in their path so that
now they mostly live on asphalt-

cement along side a few oak, pine,
the maples, and yearly shoots from
my dying bole, their saving remnant.

Turtle Island Chestnut Near Dock Ruins, Nayaug

In a few surviving clusters
and far from the maddening
city-crowd my sprouts try to

grow new trunks and branches
that flower into sweet, soft-
shelled, nuts. You didn't know

what you were doing when you
unloaded the blight from ships
on the Connecticut, felled my

siblings. Maybe you'll be more
careful, will choose to act
knowing something about not-

knowing, have realized how
fragile and sweet you are,
will survive by living gently.

Mountain Laurel, Little Moose Mountain, The Adirondacks

In spring, if you let go fear of
the tangled dark and venture in,

the understory will twinkle with
rose-pink galaxies and nectar-

clusters sprung by passing bees.
Those who ate trees just walked

by me when they walked in deep
woods around windfalls and through

bramble. They knew my leaves to
be toxic. Like them, walk on by

my evergreen branches and enjoy
day-lit stars, one of the rewards

when you give up fear, and enter.

Elm: What It Should Have Meant To Be
An American In 2003

I by the highway died but standing still
watch over you with strength, concern, and grace.

Black Spruce Bucked And Piled Outside
The Kitchen Window, Oquossoc

Heart ache in emptiness:
I was a hundred year spruce

with bent half-moon lower
boughs curving down to catch

your heart each morning when
you looked out the window

unawares, your friend rooted
in presence. Now I'm bucked

and piled over what remains
of my roots. You chain-sawed

me down because of heart-rot
and oblong slashes in my bark,

the holes a pileated drilled
for ant larvae. You feared

I'd fall on your house, didn't
know how much you'd miss me.

Now, a wraith of spirit-words
will have to console you,

create the trunk and limbs
you see when you look out

the window, be a companion
for the pained solitude of

remembering your mistake,
the ground accepting memory

that might lead you to walk
more gently on the earth.

Listen to my wraith, to what
my wood-strength honored, to

the voices of other spruce.
And along with them coyote-

laughter scaling the mountains
at night, two-leggeds talking

on your deck. When you suffer
even greater loss, the death

of a friend or loved one, hear
the whisper of a subsiding

wind, the sawing breakup of
ice in spring, the stillness

of a winter's night when, under
tinkling sky-silence, a deeper

freeze cracks and booms over
thickening lake ice, the nearly

inaudible feet-scurry of a red
squirrel over my limbs and boles

piled on the ground, my words
that come unbidden to your lips.

Ash, Wassuc

I'm clean honesty in my prime,
will cleave with ease when

split, the quietest tree
in these eastern forests.

Conifers murmur when snow
falls off in spring thankful

to be free. Maples flush
their thanks with run-off

silt turned sweet. The grain
of my wood is a forthright

'yes' and 'no' of straight
integrity that splits clear.

Tamarack, Oquossoc

I'm your need for renewal
growing between boulders

where the outlet river
from the lake used to run,

in spring budding light-
green, then deepening in

summer before falling yellow
in October, your need for

the perspective a needle-
dropping conifer offers

about river beds, cycles,
restoration, for the every-

where inhuman longing for
beauty, for the all that

draws and sheds needle-
leaves through the seasons.

Alder, Stabilizing Soil, Narramantic Island

Lush stems of everyday growth.
Without thinking abstractly
we comprehend wet earth, hold

up cellulose fiber with our
roots spread through leaf-
detritus and peat, grow from

least light, root here by
the lake or on river banks.
We intuit water and reflect

it green in heart-leafed
energy tenacious by a bog,
footpath, or ancient riverbed.

White Birch, Leaning Over The Outhouse, Oquossoc

I turn brown scrolls and curled
remembrance into enduring wood,
accept everything you let go,

absorb residue and soil, take
streams and ribbon-strips of what
you're done with and transform

them into white parchments inked
with mineral and sun. My peelings
are pages of use and what you

no longer care about, intentions
you've given up, acts that have
served their purpose, those

that have not. I leaf and grow
from what you have grown from,
provide you a balanced seeing

of everything rooted in earth-
decay, water, and the dead,
fibers of hard-wooded integrity.

White Oak, Meshomasic State Forest

Just see, stand still, be.
Keep your eyes open so you
know how snow disappears as

quietly as it came. Feel
the invisible, hear what fir
boughs say when the unseen

touches them. See again how
I lift the hidden-in-earth
sympathetically in spring

through water that flows into
branch and twig, releasing my
first shelled-red into green.

Poplar, South Bog, Oquossoc

You wonder at my splurge
of green in spring, paper-
thin yellows in fall, how
my quick roots lift suckers
into sun and grow stands
of heart-shaped leaves.

I wonder at how your brain
becomes a mind, chemicals
catalyze an intelligence
that hears a single voice
among many and sometimes
knows its limits, com-
prehends eons, an ice age,
galaxies, the infinitely
small, how it signals need,
comes to satisfaction
through the simple, connects
with other two-leggeds
and survives, though changed,
the deadpan fall of grief.
Those neurons, how amazing
when they give up trying
to control, only pulse
in cellular depths as
genes do in my roots!

Fir Brushing The Screen Of The Living Room Window, Naubuc

My vibrations have their own
frequencies: bark and needles

trembled into syllable-pitch
rising from my roots, resin-

fragrance keyed by the life-
form I live. When I speak,

hear the timbre of your faith-
ful companion and friend.

Aspen Below Kachina Peak

Below me in the plaza two-leggeds
dance like my leaves in the slightest
wind. They know that inside trust
is an ocean deeper than the grave,
more real than string theory, more
satisfying, even, than their feast.
When drumbeats carry them my leaves
tremble and the Pueblo. Their faith
in the earth vibrates with the un–
seen as torchlight and fire-circle
reach into dark corners, doorways
and over the dirt plaza shadowed
by vigas and roof-latillas where
everyone, even the old and crippled,
enters a sacred grove of friendship.

Interlude: A Responsory

A Two-Legged Falls For Trees

I'm in love with white pine,
not just the guardian who hails

me on Rt. 17 by the old exit
river to Mooselookmeguntic

but every blessed pine I hear,
those beside the grocery,

the offices of Stony Batter,
the Carry Road from Oquossoc

to Mooselook, those further
south above the Connecticut's

floodplain: Every tree loves
in return, returning the care

and thought I give, my dreams
at night of spirits holding

steady holding me: limbs
and flesh an abiding body.

How The White Pine Grieves

Quietly, with dignity, over
years, decades, sometimes
a century, flesh soft under
bark, pulling water-mineral
into the sky to be used
the following year, needles
the sharp pain of a lost
human love, my mother, bless
her heart, my mother on
the couch with a vertebra
slipped and a dialysis machine,
her life in the balance before
she died and asking with
her brown brown eyes, help
me, please my son, help me.

When Trees Stop Talking

don't stop speaking but do so
in a murmur, a whisper, a coo.
Even if you don't vocalize words,

hear them in your head and they'll
be heard by the oak or tamarack.
They'll take them under advisement

and a week or month later, even
as long as a year, they'll speak.
Stand quiet before, say, the shag-

bark with your head bowed and your
hands doing what ever they do.
Look up at the crown, then down

over strips of curled hair-bark,
black underneath with the river
below the embankment. You'll

feel tingles in your bone-fluids,
smell fragrance of companionable
wood, hear a rising of light-

vibrations from bark and ground,
then simple words, not quite
lullabies but language everyone

understands telling you to return,
keep faith, walk the straight path
and listen to unceasing rivers.

High Plains Dialogue

Near Shoshoni, the cottonwood
told the box elder she remembered
unceasing hoof beats after two-
leggeds let their four-leggeds

drink in the creek. I entered
the conversation and told them
about squealing rubber on thru-
ways and streets everywhere.

The cottonwood said she knew
about all that because she'd
guessed that the wheel would
replace hoof and foot-patter

and that two-leggeds would cut
every tree they could, pave
mountains and riverbanks, plains
and valleys with tar and asphalt.

The box elder added that even
their sister, the sagebrush,
knew what would happen, that
though thorned in sweet grass on

the bluff above it lived with
whatever us two-leggeds did,
had done so and survived through
the deep intelligence of earth.

Psalms

Weeping Birch, The Lodge Below The Big Horns

When you've not slept well,
let the first softness of

light lead you back into
down, into the warmth of

a dream where numberless
sheep gather in the draw,

where lambs loud-bleat be-
low basalt cliffs sheltered

from wind and snow. Then
dawn will be evening when

day folds into night, when
a hearth fire illuminates

stories of high plains sheep
herding, a shed and watering

hole where you can drink
satisfaction. The sun that

brings day warms the land-
scape of dreams and sleep.

Box Elder By Piney Creek

Still with samaras hanging
I watch grosbeaks, mule deer,
sometimes pronghorn, keep
my angle of perception low
and lean out in a late winter
blizzard to protect cattle
and wild turkey sheltered
below treeless hills and
worn crags, tell them how
the seeds of spring are ready
to fall, how squalls will
become transparent as earth
turns and sun warms their
bottom land, how spirits
are protected and sustained
by my leaning over them, by
the strength of my trunks
carrying samaras that help
in the great recycling
so that nothing is ever
lost in snow and blizzard.

Cottonwood, Where Clear Creek Joins Piney

Here on the high plains I
grow girth through kin-

ship with four-leggeds, willow,
many lives, your life, want

you to have the faith you
don't believe you have, want

you to be who you are, to
know that what you've come

from and lived through has
given you everything you

need, that you can release
the burden of aloneness by

drawing near without words.
I want you to understand you

are as simple as I, desiring
only to touch, be touched.

The Oldest Willow In The Willow Draw Near The Tongue

Spring green and late winter
yellow unveil anew what I've
lived and live: catkin seeds,

boughs, and cambium cells re-
plicating circumference-ringed
years just as every spring

cumulus and the broad reach of
cirrus tell of vapor-tumbled
plates under stratus-seas

surging, lava-creation piled
cloud on cloud, the towering
story of continents diving

under mountains, rocks, river
beds. If you watch the sky each
year as I have for a century,

if you walk over wind-dry foot
hills and join me, you'll look
up and see our planet folding

west to east in cell-prophecies
of thunder, in cloud-quaking
fault lines just when a lightning

strike flames a prairie fire
to the lip of the draw, witness
your story, mine, the earth's.

White Pine, The Guardian, Route 17

Roadside a snag but
still watching over you,

dead boughs and trunk
beside the road you

walk every day for mail
and friendship, when

you doubt and believe
though you have no cause

to do either, when
you despair and hope

though neither makes
a difference. Look up

as you pass and see me
rooted still and watching.

Fir On The Oquossoc Shore, Singing

My voice deepens through roots
as I grow, vibrates a base that

steadies the bite-thrust of
blizzards in winter, the heavy

heat of summer, autumn's sinking
through leaves into solitude,

spring lake-ice wind-blown onto
shore rocks where gulls and ducks

squall over newly unfrozen fish.
Year after year I reach straight

up, my trunk and voice grounded
in incremental rhythms evergreen.

Beech, The Red Hill Bluff Above The Connecticut, How I Sustain You

All winter my paper-leaves
hang like petitions in dark,

the cold I live through in-
to spring when I let go

and pull water-mineral to
my heart, medicines for

healing in the wheel of
seasons that make buds leaf

green until turning into
yellow-white prayer flags

that join the composted
health of everything that is.

Yew In The Cemetery, Naubuc

I recover everything,
bring bones and sinews

to the light, the darker
shades of what has re-

turned, lift a nail,
the swirl of thumbprint,

flesh, and cartilage,
glow blue, dark-green

by day night, and
rise beside granite

with the solid, quiet
flame of recovery.

Hornbeam, The West Shore Of The Island,
January, 2004

Do you hear me over the water
of the still unfrozen lake?
My throat-muscle doesn't make
echoes as it used to across
ice and snow in the great bowl
of ridgeline and mountain.

A Fed-Ex truck driving to
Rumford spews smoke into warm,
almost summer, air. Further
south, smoke streams from
stacks of coal-burning power
plants. Cars and trucks
exhaust the air. Loons left
only a week ago and snow
melts the day after it falls.

White Oak, Red Hill Overlooking Nayaug

Even when you are
walking away as trees

do sometimes when
they want more to

love, know you are
taken by desire for

new friends as I
am: for sugar maple,

birch, shagbark,
their climax in

summer, in winter
firm stands against

weather. When I
find my heart's

desire I root down
and leaf as you can,

hold earth-spirits
in limb and branch,

shade the downward
path to the river.

Fir By The Porch, Listening

The musician of the forest
runs beneath my boughs.
He's the little brother
of Beaver and Fox, hides
under garden boxes, darts
out to see if it's rain
or sun, carries seed-
cones between his teeth
when he isn't chattering,
caches them for winter,
accompanies Chickadee,
Waxwing, Raven in concert.
I'm rapt and thankful
that his feeding and
singing bring new green
to understory, to ledge
and ground mulch, flower-
tunes and saplings that
remind me how I got here.

Mountain Ash, Growing By The Fallen-Down Shed

I grow where no one else
chooses, near swamp, low
lying lakeland, high in

mountains on a bouldered
ledge, here by rotting
planks, studs, sheeting.

I call waxwings and others
in fall and winter, asking
with red berries. They

take what I offer and fly
back and forth singing
recitatives about fruit

and my scraggly trunk,
chromatic scales that make
the undesirable beautiful.

Beech In A Grove, Red Hill, My Roots
(beech, book: IE bhāgo)

Autumn leaves like clear
leather, pages bound in
calf and later, in winter,
the few still hanging
bleached white. Stop be-
side me on this loam-sand
bluff left by an ancient
lake. Take a moment to
read runes, parchments,
fall-dull colors of brown.
You'll enter the root of
all books, read one chapter
after another indexed
between skin-veins in
the library of the seasons.
With a staff carved from
my heart you enter life-
deposits, letters, archived
pages beyond despair on
the other side of loss.

Black Oak Beside A Midden Mound, Red Hill

The squirrel people told
me that truthfulness is
the food they cache for

winter, regret for what
they didn't cache a call to
remember and honor need.

Peach, The Orchard Behind The Cider Mill

If you hunger as well as thirst
in early autumn walk the path
up the ravine to Red Hill. My
pink blossoms will have fallen
long before. Feel the minerals
and sap that have risen behind
my bark into near heart-shaped
fruit, the sweetness of being
beyond which there's nothing.
What you want or need to know
is in cool fuzzy juice and sugar-
flesh grown into round pleasure.

Sugar Maple, The Cemetery Outside Of Oquossoc

When I look in your
eyes do I find virtue
as I do in the hardrock

next to me, a gnarled
pure beating, a sweetness,
the tang of worry boiled

away in soil-risen sap,
selfhood wiped into
clear transparency?

Do I see the beauty of
beginnings distilled
into the about-to-be,

the clarity of strength
when you've left behind
little fears even as

I see in shimmering
fire-lit water the flame
that gives you a soul?

Yellow Birch, The Driveway Up From The Landing

Curled grain locked into the earth
when my roots grew down over a dead
spruce, made an arch of invitation
that remained after the spruce

decayed, a choral song welcoming
whatever comes, years and years
of ringed strength grown into
old age before being cut, split,

and burned in a wood stove or open
fire. Sign of commitment and power,
being here season after season
though no stronger than any life

form: moss, club fir, even sand,
rock, and soil. But special in
that nowhere will be found my
courtesy and lesson in manners.

Bing Cherry, The Orchard By Lake Erie

Sweet singing is as sweet
as tasting and eating my

flesh, though it goes deeper
into the soul than I do.

It touches your will just
as water and sun touch my

pit which grows a thread
in the earth and, after

a few years, a stem clothed
in pink-white flowers

which later become black-
purple droplets. Music

touches volition, yours,
mine, that of others.

It gives a dark-sweet,
radiant desire for change.

White Cedar Looking West Towards Mooselook:
Its Witness

I feed through roots on
fallen spruce and fir in
this lakeside bog, feel

no guilt as you do, keep
conscience clear by letting
summer pass into fall when

I release green-latticed
berries. When winter arrives,
slithering rain and flaked

snow-crusts slide off my
limbs and leaves with ease.
Then I look up to higher

ground where hardwoods en-
dure, each of us accepting
change without remorse.

Pin Cherry Under Fir And Spruce, Oquossoc

Sweet and tough, a trickle,
a stream, intelligent in
each sapling and cell, each

pink flower on the brink
or leaves deepening yellow
in fall, in umber-red bark

protecting wood: I choose
the understory but reach
through gaps in the larger

canopy with the warmth of
imaginative understanding.
I flow whole by division

into new cells, into trunk
and crown as I create and
nurture tiny plenitudes.

Fir Sapling, Aziscohos After Clear-Cutting

I'm balsam, heart wood, resin-
balm, a little healing after

you two-leggeds have sprayed
herbicides on hardwood saplings.

You kill them because you want
me for pulp on land your feller-

bunchers will clear. But I grow
a fiber of strength no matter

what and rise on this hillside
of northern air aflower with

cones, seeds, and herbal fragrance,
trying to make our forest whole.

Pear Looking East Above The Connecticut

I mark revolutions by
the shapes I give each
round turning, slide
sweetly in the dead
of winter into the new
year when deer walk
on snow-cover leaving
bitten-off saplings
of birch and alder,
black-brown droppings
on white. Do you realize
you have no words for
passings big and small?
For circles the globe
makes under the friendly
plumbed moon and grand-
mother sun? I have my
way of marking each
season, each turning
that moves brown into
green ripening, then
back into brown, of
shaking the fragile:
my petals that prepare
for the sweet flesh
of autumn, dear wind-
falls, when you taste

fragrant, tear-dropped
juice rounded into
dreams as you eat plump
fruit from my boughs
in bell-shaped wonder.

Rhododendron, Oquossoc, By The Cabin

After two leggeds had planted
me by the walk, spider-woman
stopped and told me how every

design is a path leading to
simplicity, pattern a template
for the circle all lines end

in, symmetry a vibration of
dew in morning sunlight co-
incident with the rustle of

leaves. She said she is part
of a family, that her younger
brother burrows under ground,

an older catches a trout with
his talons, another walks high
trails and butts his horns

to call the air to worship,
that, of her many sisters,
one makes a den in a culvert,

another sleeps winter in
a cave, another spends summer
eating swamp-grass in the bog,

that the web she weaves be-
tween my evergreen leaves
and branches is the same web

that holds stars in their
galaxies, binds electrons
and atoms into the universe.

Red Oak Rooted On Red Hill Above The Floodplain

I will be here long
after you're gone, after
your two-legged life ends
where it began, after
measurements no longer
measure anything, after
what you hadn't thought
to watch for arrives,
after storms cease and
stillness leaves earth
ready to be born anew.

White Pine After Living A Hundred Years
Looking West Across The Lake

Night doesn't fall, as you say
it does, but rises. It gathers
in shadows of rock and stump,
mills under club spruce, fern,
rhododendron before seeping out
of peat beneath my brothers
and sisters, clings to my trunk
and snagged lower branches,
spills over woodyard, garden,
then, after reaching out with
gray fingers over black waters,
condenses under autumn-dark
birch and maple on the far
shore, closes in on a house,
a two-legged in white-wool
sweater carrying a rocker
indoors, bedroom window be-
hind the porch a yellow glow
in the half-log wall, easily
and simply rises into air and
softly, even quickly, trans-
forms the sky which turns into
dark beneath leaving a star
that foretells the birth of light.

Coda

Earth Voice

The trees have spoken. Now go,
listen to the mountains,
winged-feather

spirits, four-leggeds, even
scale-bodies athrob
in water.

Go, listen to all creature-
beings, not just
to the white

pine, ash, and spruce but to
the turn of seasons,
lake-murmur

below lake shine, soil-loam
and layers of stone.
You'll think

in veins deep down and connect
to the ground you
grow from,

speak the tongue of gratitude,
be a two-legged who
has a mind.

    Go, listen

Notes:

"The Voice Of Earth" — for Linda & Bill Burk

"Lodgepole By The Medicine
 Wheel" — for Elizabeth Tiedens,

"White Cedar, A Medicine Chest
 Beside Oquossoc Waters" — for Joan Malerba-Foran

"Silver Maple Rooted Though A
 Granite Crevice, Cupsuptic" — for Jamie Taylor

"Sumac, The Floodplain, Nayaug" — for Sophie Wadsworth

"White Birch Sapling In Peat
 Beside Gray Water, Oquossoc" — for Anne Roundy

"Plum, The Orchard
 In The Wassuc Hills" — for Ruth Alexander

"Shagbark Above An Oxbow In
 The Connecticut — for Dave Ahlgren

"Apple In The Orchard Off The
 Turnpike,Naubuc" — for Eleanor Godway

"Eastern Hemlock By A Writer's
 Studio Above The Connecticut" — for Susan Baillet &
 Herman Asarnow

"Douglas Fir, The Inland Passage,
 Kilkatla" — for Tia & Tom Thornton

"Mountain Laurel, Little Moose
 Mountain, The Adirondacks" — for Lynn Johnson

"Elm: What It Should Have Meant
 To Be An American In 2003" — for Fred Pfeil

"Black Spruce Bucked And Piled
 Outside The Kitchen Window,
 Oquossoc" — for Diane & Steve
 Foley

"White Birch Leaning Over The
 Outhouse, Oquossoc" — for Linda & Kit Casper

"White Oak, Meshomasic State
    Forest"   for Emily Chasse
"Beech, The Red Hill Bluff Above
    The Connecticut,How I Sustain
    You"   for Pam Nomura
"Beech In A Grove, Red Hill,
    My Roots   for Jeffrey Kaimowitz
"Yellow Birch, The Driveway Up
    From The Landing"   for Martha & John
                                      Bicknell

"Bing Cherry, The Orchard
    By Lake Erie"   for Dave Briggs
"Pin Cherry Under Fir And
    Spruce, Oquossoc"   for Georgene & Mike
                                      Skahill
"Fir Sapling, Aziscohos After Clear
    Cutting"   for Carol & Jeff
                                      Ellinwood

"Pear Looking East Above
    The Connecticut"   for Judy Moran
"Rhododendron, Oquossoc,
    By The Cabin"   for Mary Kramer &
                                      Arthur Feinsod

"White Pine, After Living A
    Hundred Years Looking West
    Across The Lake"   for Wess Connally
"Earth Voice"   for Anna Moberly

About The Author

Hugh Ogden is the author of four other books of poems (most recently, BRINGING A FIR STRAIGHT DOWN) and two chapbooks. His poetry reading is on a CD and tape. Among his awards are a National Endowment For The Arts Fellowship and three grants from the Connecticut Commission On The Arts. He's been a Fellow at the MacDowell Colony twice and won residencies at The Island Institute, Hawthornden Castle, and Le Château de Lavigny, as well as other artist colonies. He's taught at Trinity College for 39 years where he co-founded the Creative Writing program. He also founded the Creative Writing Program at the Academy For The Arts in Hartford (a magnet high school) where he teaches poetry workshops. Before coming to Trinity, he taught Greek and Latin literature for seven years in the Honors Program at the University of Michigan. He's worked with grade school children, the elderly, handicapped, and people in prisons and lived or spent time on Reservations and Pueblos throughout the West. He lives in Glastonbury, CT and on an island in a northwest Maine mountain lake.